Ellis Island

THE OFFICIAL SOUVENIR GUIDE

By Colin Hamblin
Additional text by Barry Moreno

Front and Back Cover:
Photos by Joe Luman © Terrell Creative
Historical Photo Courtesy Library of Congress

With thanks to the dedicated
National Park Service staff
at Ellis Island — especially
Diana Pardue, Barry Moreno,
and Brian Feeney — for their
timely assistance with this
project, and to Klaus Schnitzer
for sharing his photographic
insights of Ellis Island.

Printed by Terrell Creative
www.terrellcreative.com

Edited by Jane Freeburg & Barry Moreno
© 2006 Designed in USA by Terrell Creative
09K0008 • Printed in China

ISBN 13: 978-1-56944-405-4

Contents

Photo by Joe Luman © Terrell Creative

Courtesy Library of Congress

Chapter One
ELLIS ISLAND'S STORY

*E*llis Island is a place of names. Here, millions of immigrants called out theirs for the first time — proud names, long names, names that would twist the tongue — before they stepped ashore onto America's soil. To most, Ellis Island was an Isle of Hope, a brief stopping point on the way to a better life. To an unfortunate few, it became an Isle of Tears, a place of detention and possible rejection. Ellis Island, and its names, reflect its story.

In the 17th century, when the Dutch controlled New York — then known as New Amsterdam — Ellis Island was called *Kioshk* or Gull Island by the Mohegan (or Mohican) Indians who lived along the Hudson River. The Indians named the small sandbank for the waterbirds which crowded its shores. Michael Paauw, a Dutchman who purchased the island from the local inhabitants in the 1630s, renamed it Oyster Island for the rich beds of shellfish which encircled it. During the next century the island passed through many hands as the title to

not only New York but to the United States was contested. Locals coined the name Gibbet Island for pirates that were hung there, but it wasn't until the 1780s that Samuel Ellis, the island's permanent namesake, came to own the property.

Ellis developed the island as a recreation and picnic spot and even kept a large "pleasure sleigh" there. In 1788 Ellis' family sold the property for $3,200 to John A. Berry, the last private owner before the United States War Department, nervous about the international tensions of the Napoleonic Wars, purchased the island for $10,000 in June of 1808. Ellis Island, as it continued to be called, was to be the site of Fort Gibson, one of a number of fortifications built just before the War of 1812 as part of New York City's first line of defense. The other constructions included Fort Wood on Bedloe's Island (now Liberty Island), and Castle Clinton, which stood three hundred feet off the shore of the Battery at the southern tip of Manhattan.

➤ *Landing at Ellis Island*

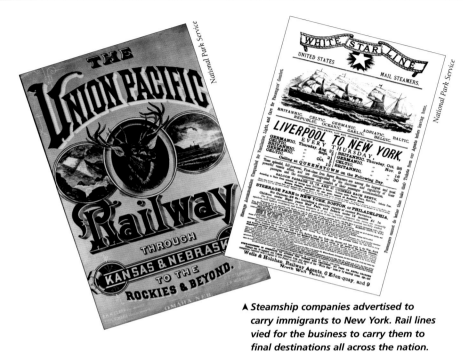

National Park Service

▲ **Steamship companies advertised to carry immigrants to New York. Rail lines vied for the business to carry them to final destinations all across the nation.**

Although the British blockaded the harbor for over a year, New York's fortifications never saw any action. Fort Gibson, however, was used to detain the prisoners of war, a haunting premonition of one of Ellis Island's recurring and unfortunate roles.

After the War of 1812 ended, Ellis Island remained largely deserted until the 1830s when the Navy built a powder magazine on the island. Actively used during the Civil War, this munitions dump became the focus of public protest for years to come. In 1868 *The Sun* and *Harper's Weekly* ran articles about "the imminent peril of being at once destroyed by the explosions of the magazines on Ellis Island," and in 1876, Representative Augustus A. Hardenburg of New Jersey stated that "if it were struck by lightning, the shock would destroy Jersey City, Hoboken, and parts of New York." Although Fort Gibson had been officially dismantled in 1861, not until 1890 did Congress

adopt legislation to clear the island of munitions. Before the bill passed it was amended to include an appropriation of $75,000 for "improving Ellis Island for immigration purposes." On April 11, 1890, President Benjamin Harrison signed the legislation into law.

The need for an immigration depot had first been voiced by the New York Commissioner of Immigration in 1847 when a severe potato famine in Ireland sent thousands of starving immigrants streaming into New England and New York. His request to use the old fort on Ellis Island to house "convalescent emigrants" was politely denied: Ellis Island's immigration history would come later. Government officials chose instead Castle Garden as the nation's first immigration depot.

Decommissioned in 1823, the old fort known as Castle Clinton had been renamed Castle Garden and converted into a concert hall where such dignitaries as Marquis de Lafayette and President Andrew Jackson were entertained. The hall received international attention in 1850 when famous opera singer and Swedish immigrant Jenny Lind performed there under the billing of P.T. Barnum. By 1855, however, the state became more concerned with counting heads than ticket stubs.

Immigration to the United States had increased, and both state and federal governments sought a way to regulate the flow, as well as profit from it. Along with their bundled possessions, newcomers to America brought skilled hands and able bodies. Some saw this human influx as a boon to the work force and economy of a fledgling nation. Others saw immigrants as merely hungry mouths and charity cases which would drain the U.S. Treasury. A report by Representative Melbourne Ford of Michigan in the 1880s concluded that New York State annually expended 20 million dollars "in taking care of paupers [and] insane

National Park Service

◄ **Castle Garden served as America's immigration depot from 1855-1890.**

▼ **Castle Clinton in Battery Park**

National Park Service

persons … and that this condition of affairs is due largely to improper immigration." In response to these prevailing sentiments, Congress drafted a flurry of legislation — laws that became benchmarks against which an immigrant was measured during the inspection process.

The first two laws, passed in 1882, included the Chinese Exclusion Act, which banned Chinese immigration and denied citizenship to those already in the U.S. The first general federal immigration law denied entrance to "any convict, lunatic, idiot, or any person unable to take care of himself or herself without becoming a public charge." In 1891 this law was expanded to include the expulsion of paupers, prostitutes, polygamists, or "persons suffering from loathsome or a dangerous contagious disease." Other legislation included the Alien Contract Labor Law, passed in 1885 under pressure from the labor unions, as an attempt to protect American workers from industrialists who imported immigrant labor to break strikes or lower wages.

While these laws were meant to protect the immigrant as well as the American citizen, they had little effect in deterring swindlers, runners, and labor brokers from exploiting new arrivals after they passed through the gates at Castle Garden. Accounts of abuse and inhumane treatment inside the depot triggered newspaper accounts, such as Joseph Pulitzer's exposé for *The World*, which accused the registry clerks and commissioners at Castle Garden of corruption and criminal activity. As the newspaper accounts grew, so did the embarrassment of the federal government, and in February of 1890, the Treasury Department, then responsible for immigration affairs, cancelled their contract with the New York State immigration commissioners, thereby transferring full responsibility for inspecting immigrants to the federal government. Construction of a new depot was to begin immediately — preferably on an island site, where an immigrant could be protected, guided, and if needed, easily detained.

Source Unknown

◄ *The first immigration station buildings on Ellis Island were destroyed by a fire in 1897.*

Governor's Island was the first choice, but the War Department refused to give up any part of it. Public outcry over dumping "Europe's garbage" on Bedloe's Island at the foot of the Statue of Liberty (inaugurated October 28, 1886) was so great that tiny Ellis Island was finally selected even though the surrounding waters were too shallow to dock boats of any draft there.

Using ballast from incoming ships as landfill, workers doubled the island's size from its original 3.3 acres. A ferry slip was dredged, and on New Year's Day of 1892, fifteen-year-old Annie Moore from County Cork, Ireland became the first immigrant to enter the Ellis Island station. Ellis Island's immigration commissioner John B. Weber presented young Annie with a ten-dollar gold piece which she quickly palmed, wide-eyed and full of wonder.

Ellis Island's two-story building, built of Georgia pine at a cost of $200,000, was designed to process up to ten thousand immigrants a day. *Harper's Weekly* favorably described the new depot as having the appearance of a "latter-day watering place hotel, presenting to the viewer a great many-windowed expanse of buff-painted wooden walls, of blue-slate roofing, and of light and picturesque towers."

Despite its initial praise, though, the station did not age well. Five years and 1.5 million immigrants later the depot showed signs of hard use and disrepair. When a fire originating in the furnace room caused the depot to burn to the ground on June 15, 1897, Joseph Senner, commissioner of immigration at the time, commented only "a row of unsightly ramshackle tinderboxes has been removed, and when the government rebuilds we'll be forced to put up decent fireproof structures."

Although 140 immigrants and a number of employees were on Ellis Island at the time of the fire, no one was injured. But a large number of immigration records were lost, further pressuring the federal government to rebuild the depot with fireproof materials. Later that year Congress earmarked $600,000 to begin construction.

The new depot would be one of the first major government buildings commissioned under competitive procedures mandated by the Tarsney Act. Although a number of large and prestigious firms submitted bids, including McKim, Mead & White and Carrere & Hastings, the small architectural firm Boring and Tilton landed the contract to rebuild Ellis Island's Immigration Center.

▲ *Ellis Island's main building as it appeared circa 1910. Roof gardens on both the east and west wings were replaced by the third floor dormitories and offices by 1911.*

When Boring & Tilton submitted their General Plan in 1898, it included a hospital complex situated on a second adjoining island, to be created from landfill excavated from the construction of New York City's fledgling subway system. The central focus of their plan was the award-winning immigrant inspection station. The building's French Renaissance exterior of brick with limestone trim received praise at three World's Fairs and was awarded the Gold Medal at the Paris Exhibition of 1900.

Although the interior plan was thought to be well organized for the purposes of immigration inspection, the station was designed to process only 500,000 immigrants a year. As immigration had tapered off in the 1890s to around 250,000 immigrants annually, officials assumed the facilities would be more than adequate. No one could have guessed at the huge number of immigrants that were about to knock on America's door.

While the station was to take only twelve months to build, strikes, contract disputes, and a lack of skilled laborers delayed work and inflated construction costs to over $1,000,000. When the main building finally opened on December 17, 1900, the *New York Times* described Ellis Island's Immigration Station as "an imposing as well as a pleasing addition to the picturesque waterfront metropolis … [where] five thousand persons can be thoroughly examined with perfect ease."

The first day of operation, 2,251 people were inspected on Ellis Island — immigrants "ranging in age from three months to three score and ten," as one newspaper reported. In just six years, however, the number of hopeful new Americans who climbed the steep slate stairs to the great Registry Room would increase from 389,000 in 1901 to just over one million in 1907, America's peak immigration year.

Photo by Joe Luman © Terrell Creative

Immigration to the United States through Ellis Island and All Entry Ports, 1903-24

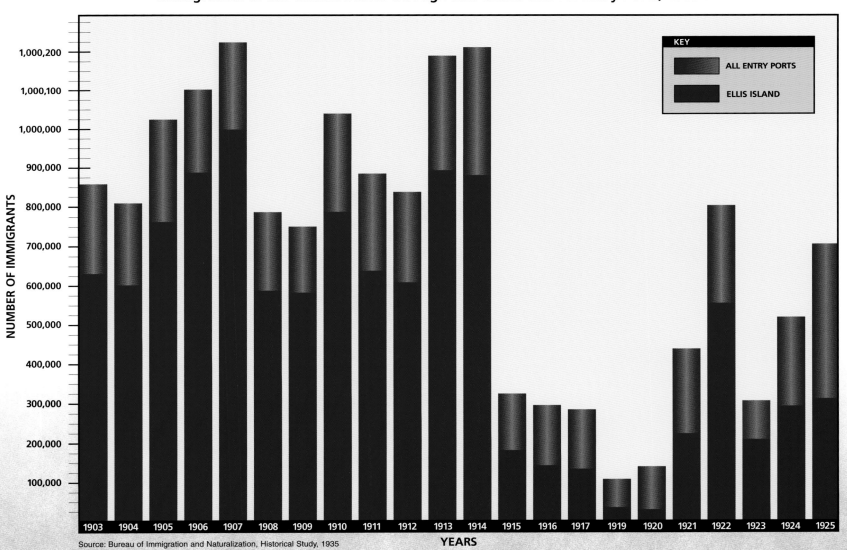

Source: Bureau of Immigration and Naturalization, Historical Study, 1935

Augustus Sherman Collection/National Park Service

Chapter Two
THE IMMIGRATION EXPERIENCE

When the great steamships of the early 20th century sailed into New York Harbor, the faces of a thousand nations were on board. A broad, beaming, multicolored parade, these were the immigrants of the world: there were bearded Russian Jews, Irish farmers whose hands were weathered like the land they had left, Greeks in foustanelas and slippers, Italians with waxed moustaches, Cossacks with elegantly crafted swords, English in short knickers, and Arabs in long robes. The Old World lay behind them. Ahead was a new life, huge and promising. Gone were the autocracies and kings, the systems of caste and peasantry, of famine and numbing poverty. But also left behind were friends and family, as well as tradition and customs generations old.

As anchors slid into the harbor silt, and whistles blew in rival chorus, this multitude clambered up from the steerage decks to fashion in their minds forever their first glimpse of America. The city skyline loomed over them like a great, blocky mountain range. Poet Walt Whitman described New York as the "City of the World (for all races are here, all the lands of the earth make contributions here:) City of the sea! City of hurried and glittering tides! City whose gleeful tides continually rush and recede, whirling in and out with eddies and foam! City of wharves and stores — city of tall façades of marble and iron! Proud and passionate city — mettlesome, mad, extravagant, city!"

Below, the harbor teemed with activity as tugboats churned river water and dockhands wrestled cargo at America's most populous port. Across the Hudson stood the mythic vision of America: salt-green and copper-clad, the Statue of Liberty offered a mute but powerful welcome.

➤ *Gypsy family from Serbia*

◄ *Immigrants at Ellis Island*

13

National Park Service

In the shadow of all the activity, on the New Jersey side of the river, were the red brick buildings of Ellis Island. The four towers of its largest building rose over 140 feet into the air, punctuating its already intimidating façade with ram-rod sternness. This was an official building, a place of rules and questions, of government and bureaucracy, where five thousand people a day were processed.

Men usually immigrated first, to find jobs and housing. Later they would send for their wives, children, and parents as part of the largest mass movement of people in world history. In all, close to 60 million people sought to find new opportunities during the 19th and early 20th centuries. Some merely crossed borders in Europe but many headed for countries such as Australia, New Zealand, Brazil, Argentina, and Canada. The majority, however, headed to the United States where they heard promise for jobs, freedom, and fortune to be made. In the hundred years previous to 1924, when the country's open door abruptly shut, 34 million immigrants landed on America's soil.

The earliest influx of new arrivals started in the mid 1840s when Europe felt the throes of a bitter famine. This First Wave of immigrants — primarily Northern Europeans from Ireland, England, Germany, and Scandinavia — fled starvation, conservative governments, and the social upheaval brought about by the Industrial Revolution. A Second Wave of immigrants streamed out of Southern and Eastern

Courtesy Library of Congress

Europe from 1890-1924, accounting for the flood tide of new arrivals during America's peak immigration years. Along with fleeing the burden of high taxes, poverty, and overpopulation, these "new" immigrants were also victims of oppression and religious persecution. Jews living in Romania, Russia, and Poland were being driven from their homes by a series of pogroms, riots, and discriminatory laws enforced by authoritarian governments. Similarly the Croats and the Serbs in Hungary, the Poles in Germany, and the Irish persecuted under English rule all saw America as a land of freedom, as well as opportunity.

▲ **German passengers bound for America, circa 1904**
➤ **The excitement builds for first class passengers as they reach America.**

PASSAGE ACROSS THE ATLANTIC

Augustus Sherman Collection/National Park Service

By the 1880s steam-powered ships had modernized the business of ocean travel, replacing sailing vessels and cutting the time to make the Atlantic crossing from three months to two weeks. Large shipping lines such as Cunard and White Star competed fiercely for the emigrants, who were seen as profitable, self-loading cargo. Huge floating villages, the steamships could accommodate as many as two thousand passengers in steerage, so called because it was located on the lower decks where the steering mechanism of the sailing ships had once been housed. These long narrow compartments were divided into separate dormitories for single men, single women, and families. Jammed with metal-framed berths three bunks high, the air in steerage became rank with the heavy odor of spoiled food, seasickness, and unwashed bodies. There was little privacy, and the lack of adequate toilet facilities made it difficult to keep clean. Sophia Kreitzberg, a Russian Jew who emigrated in 1908, recalled

that "the atmosphere was so thick and dense with smoke and bodily odors that your head itched, and when you went to scratch your head … you got lice in your hands."

Gradually conditions improved for emigrant passengers. By 1910 many ships had replaced steerage with four- and six-berth third class cabins. These vessels served meals in dining rooms with long tables set with dishes and utensils. On many of the older ships, however, passengers still ate meals from a tin mess kit while sitting on deck or in the hot cramped steerage dormitories. "We had a bucket with four or five compartments in it," remembers F. G. Gregot, who immigrated from Lithuania in 1914. "They'd put their food in them compartments. You put a lid on it. And put another compartment on top of that … until we finally got all we was suppose to get."

The Italian lines served pasta and wine, and many shipping lines provided kosher food for Jewish passengers, but not all ships catered to ethnic or religious tastes. Cases of malnutrition were not uncommon. Standard fare consisted of potatoes, soup, eggs, fish, stringy meat, prunes — and whatever foods the immigrants carried from home. "[It was] a noisy, picturesque, garlicky crowd on the steerage deck," recalled Louis Adamic, a Slovenian immigrant in 1913. "[There were] people of perhaps a dozen nationalities."

By the time the steamships sailed into the Upper Bay, first and second-class passengers had already been inspected and cleared to land by immigration officials who had come on board from Quarantine at the Hudson River's mouth. Steerage passengers, however, were afforded no such privileges and their first steps on the mainland were brief. Disembarking on the Hudson River piers, they were summarily directed helter-skelter onto ferries which shuttled them to Ellis Island.

▲ *A family of thirteen from the Netherlands*

➤ *Mother and her 11 children from Holland, on their way to Minnesota*

▼ *Ferry docks with new arrivals at Ellis Island*

Augustus Sherman Collection/National Park Service

Courtesy Library of Congress

Chartered by the steamship companies, these vessels were little better than open-air barges, freezing in the winter, sweltering hot in the summer, and lacking toilet facilities and life-saving equipment. Deaths caused by exposure to cold were not uncommon and one Public Health Service official estimated that of the children suffering from measles when they arrived, thirty percent subsequently died because of their trip across the harbor. Although the ferries were thought adequate for the short ride, busy days saw immigrants imprisoned on these vessels for hours while they waited their turn to land at Ellis Island. The harbor was often choked with steamships crammed with as many as twenty thousand passengers waiting to disembark and be ferried to Ellis Island. Sometimes new arrivals had to wait in steerage for days, prolonging the miserable journey, and making America's promise that much more elusive.

THE INSPECTION PROCESS

When they landed, the immigrants had numbered tags pinned to their clothes which indicated the manifest page and line number on which their names appeared. These numbers were later used by immigration inspectors to cross-reference immigrants about their right to land. Anna Vida, a Hungarian immigrant in 1921, comically remembers the sight: "We had all sorts of tags on us …We must have looked like marked-down merchandise at Gimbel's basement store or something."

Though relatively few immigrants who landed at Ellis Island were denied entry, the two percent that were excluded often equaled over a thousand people a month during peak immigration years. The Ellis Island processing station was meant to channel and filter the seemingly endless supply of human energy that came to fuel America's burgeoning economy, and everywhere on the island there was an air of purpose. Greeted with pointing fingers and unintelligible commands, the new arrivals formed a line which stretched from Ellis Island dock into the Baggage Room of the Main Building, winding its way up to the second floor where the immigrants were met by a team of doctors and inspectors who would decide which way the Golden Door would swing. Jostling three abreast, the immigrants made their way up the steep flight of stairs and into the great hall of the Registry Room. Although many did not know it, the inspection process had already begun.

National Park Service

▲ *Immigrants meet the team of doctors … the inspection process begins.*

Doctors inspect for Trachoma.

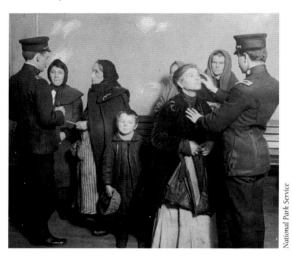

National Park Service

Courtesy Library of Congress

Scanning the moving line for signs of illness, Public Health Service doctors looked to see if anyone wheezed, coughed, shuffled, or limped as they climbed the steep ascent. Children were asked their names to make sure they weren't deaf or dumb, and those that looked over two years old were taken from their mothers' arms and made to walk.

As the line moved forward, doctors had only a few seconds to examine each immigrant, checking for sixty symptoms, from anemia to varicose veins, which might indicate a wide variety of diseases, disabilities, and physical conditions. Of primary concern were cholera, favus (scalp and nail fungus), insanity, and mental impairments. In

1907 legislation further barred immigrants suffering from tuberculosis, epilepsy, and the physically disabled.

The disease which resulted in the most exclusions, however, was trachoma, a highly contagious eye infection that could cause blindness and death. At the time, the disease was common in Southern and Eastern Europe, but relatively unknown in the U.S. (A Japanese immigrant later discovered the cure.) Physicians checked for trachoma by turning the eyelid inside out with their fingers, a hairpin, or a buttonhook to look for inflammations on the inner eyelid — a short but extremely painful experience. The "buttonhook men" were the most dreaded officials on Ellis Island.

During line inspection, those immigrants who appeared sick or were suffering from a contagious disease were marked with blue chalk and detained for further medical examination. The sick were taken to Ellis Island Hospital for observation and care, and once recovered, could proceed with their legal inspection. Those with incurable or disabling ailments, however, were excluded and returned to their port of departure at the expense of the steamship line on which they arrived. In an attempt to discourage steamship companies from transporting ill, disabled, or impoverished passengers, an immigration law of 1903 imposed a hundred-dollar fine for every excluded passenger.

Medical officers developed a letter code to indicate further inspection; roughly two out of every ten immigrants received mystifying chalk marks. This alphabet of ailments ranged from *Pg* for pregnant to *K* for hernia and *Ft* for feet. Those suspected of having feeble minds were chalked with an *X*, and along with those marked for physical ailments, about nine out of every hundred immigrants were detained for mental examination and further questioning. Usually this consisted of standard intelligence tests in which immigrants were asked to solve simple arithmetic problems, count backwards from twenty, or complete a puzzle. In an attempt to deal with immigrants' cultural differences, Ellis Island's doctors developed their own tests which allowed them to base their decision on problem solving, behavior, attitude, and the immigrant's ability to acquire knowledge. Requiring immigrants to copy geometric shapes, for instance, was only useful for testing those who had some schooling and were used to holding a pencil. Favored were visual comparison and mimicry tests which did not have to be explained by an interpreter, nor did an immigrant have to know how to read and write to solve them.

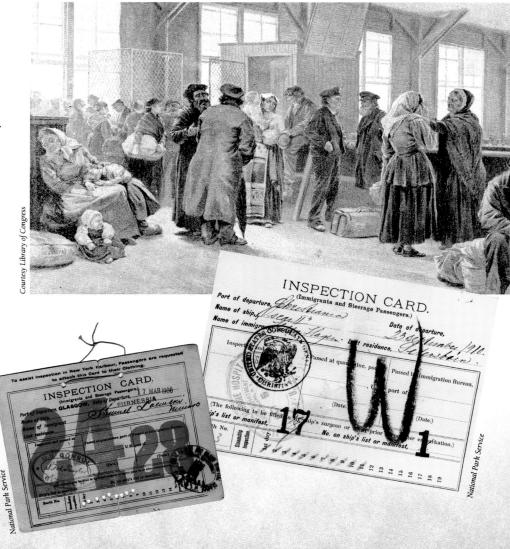

▼ *Detained immigrants on Ellis Island*

Courtesy Library of Congress

National Park Service

National Park Service

▲ *Inspection cards issued to each steerage passenger were checked and stamped by Ellis Island officials.*

➤ *Ellis Island's Registry Room in 1903*
▼ *An Irish immigrant's passport*

National Park Service

National Park Service

National Park Service

After passing the line inspection, immigrants were waved forward toward the main part of the Registry Room. There they entered a maze of open passageways and metal railings which divided the entire floor. As crowded as a country town on market day, the great hall was "a place of Babel" where all languages of the world seemed to cry out at once.

At the far end of the Registry Hall the immigration inspectors stood behind tall desks, assisted by interpreters fluent in major languages and a good many obscure dialects as well. Although the interrogation that immigrants were to face lasted only a matter of minutes, it took an average of five hours to pass through the inspection process at Ellis Island.

◄ *Guadeloupe woman*

▼ *Slovakian women*

▲ *Romanian shepherds*

Augustus Sherman Collection/National Park Service

Augustus Sherman Collection/National Park Service

Augustus Sherman Collection/National Park Service

▼ *Greek immigrants*

Augustus Sherman Collection/National Park Service

21

National Park Service

➤ *Physical examination of female immigrants*

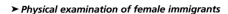

Wearing starched collars and heavy serge jackets, the inspectors verified twenty-nine bits of information already contained on the manifest sheet. Finally names were recorded with care — especially if they were spelled Andrjuljawierjus, Grzyszczyszn, or Zoutsoghianopoulas. Firing questions at the immigrants, the inspector asked them their age, occupation, marital status, and destination in an attempt to determine their social, economic, and moral fitness.

Influenced by American welfare agencies that claimed to be overwhelmed by requests for aid from impoverished immigrants, the exclusion of those "liable to become a public charge" became a cornerstone of immigration policy as early as 1882. The Alien Contract Labor Law of 1885 also excluded all immigrants who took a job in exchange for passage. Together these laws presented the immigrant with a delicate task of convincing the legal inspectors that they were strong, intelligent, and resourceful enough to find work easily, without admitting that a relative had a job waiting for them.

In 1917 anti-immigration forces succeeded in pressuring the government to impose a literacy test as a further means of restricting immigration. The law required all immigrants sixteen years or older to read a forty-word passage in their native language. Those from the Punjab district of Afghanistan, for instance, had to follow a series of printed commands, such as picking up a pencil and handing it to the immigration inspectors. Most immigrants, however, had to read biblical translations such as "Your riches are corrupted, and your garments moth-eaten. Your gold and silver is cankered; and the rust of them shall be a witness against you, and shall eat your flesh as it were fire" (James 5:2,3), which was the requisite passage for Serbians.

Augustus Sherman Collection/National Park Service

▲ *The Great Hall as seen from the west balcony, pre-1916*

Courtesy Library of Congress

◄ *Immigrants in line at Ellis Island*

Working from 9 a.m. to 7 p.m., seven days a week, each inspector questioned four hundred to five hundred immigrants a day. Those who failed to prove they were "clearly and beyond a doubt entitled to land" were detained for a hearing before the Board of Special Inquiry. As immigrants did not have the legal right to enter the U.S., there could be no lawyer present at this hearing, but friends and relatives could testify on an immigrant's behalf. The Board reviewed about seventy thousand cases a year, admitting five out of every six detainees. Those rejected could appeal the decision directly to the Secretary of Commerce and Labor in Washington, D.C. At this stage immigrants could hire a lawyer or offer a bond guaranteeing they would not become a public charity.

Along with medical detentions and immigrants facing hearing from the Board, unescorted women and children were detained until their safety was assured through the arrival of a telegram, letter, or prepaid ticket from a waiting relative. Furthermore, immigration officials

◄ *Ellis Island's dining room provided thousands of meals for the many immigrants whose stay lasted hours, days, or weeks.*

▼ *President William Howard Taft on his visit to Ellis Island on October of 1910*

refused to send single women into the streets alone, nor could they leave with a man not related to them. Fiancées, reunited with their intended husbands often married on the spot.

During peak immigration years, detentions at Ellis Island ran as high as twenty percent — thousands of immigrants a day. A detainee's stay could last days or even weeks, and accommodations were in constant shortage. From 1900-1908 dormitories consisted of two long, narrow rooms which ran along either side of the Registry Room mezzanine. Each room slept three hundred people in triple-tiered bunks (much like steerage) that could be raised, converting the rooms into daytime waiting areas. In 1906 Commissioner Robert Watchorn seriously considered hiring barges to serve as extra detention space until an appropriation of $400,000 from Congress allowed him to begin construction of the new Baggage and Dormitory Building. However, this facility was not completed until 1910. In 1907, Ellis Island's peak immigration year, 195,540 people were detained.

▼ *Train depot, not in use*

Photo by Joe Luman © Terrell Creative

Photo by Joe Luman © Terrell Creative

National Park Service

National Park Service

National Park Service

After inspection, immigrants descended from the Registry Room down the "Stairs of Separation," so called because they marked the parting of the way for many family and friends with different destinations. Immigrants were directed toward the railroad ticket office and trains to points west, or to the island's hospital and detention rooms. Those immigrants bound for Manhattan met their relatives at the "kissing post," where many joyous and tearful reunions occurred. Katherine Beychok, a Russian Jewish immigrant in 1910, remembers, "I saw a man coming forward and he was so beautiful. I didn't know he was my father … Later on I realized why he looked so familiar to me. He looked exactly like I did … But that's when I met him for the first time. And I fell in love with him and he with me."

▲ *Railroad companies, eager for settlers to populate the west, advertised farmland and work opportunities for immigrants.*

▼ *Hospital Room*

Courtesy Library of Congress

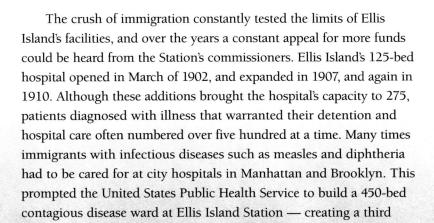

Courtesy Library of Congress

The crush of immigration constantly tested the limits of Ellis Island's facilities, and over the years a constant appeal for more funds could be heard from the Station's commissioners. Ellis Island's 125-bed hospital opened in March of 1902, and expanded in 1907, and again in 1910. Although these additions brought the hospital's capacity to 275, patients diagnosed with illness that warranted their detention and hospital care often numbered over five hundred at a time. Many times immigrants with infectious diseases such as measles and diphtheria had to be cared for at city hospitals in Manhattan and Brooklyn. This prompted the United States Public Health Service to build a 450-bed contagious disease ward at Ellis Island Station — creating a third contiguous island — as well as a psychopathic ward and a morgue.

▲ *Hospital buildings as they look today*
➤*Hospital at Ellis Island*

"[The Island] is at once a maternity ward and an insane asylum," remarked one doctor. By 1911 more than fifteen buildings at Ellis Island were devoted to medical care. Forty doctors, proficient in dealing with illness ranging from slight injuries to rare tropical diseases, staffed its hospital.

During its half-century of operation over 3,500 immigrants died at Ellis Island (including 1,400 children) and over 350 babies were born. There were also three suicides. While the 700 doctors, nurses, inspectors, interpreters, matrons, stenographers, and other staff employed during the station's peak years generally followed "Commissioner William Williams' directive to treat immigrants with kindness and consideration," the process of inspection and detention — and the frightening prospect of exclusion — remained overwhelming.

CLOSING THE OPEN DOOR

When the United States entered World War I in 1917, anti-immigration sentiment and isolationist hostilities were at their highest. Congress had just passed legislation, over the veto of President Woodrow Wilson, requiring immigrants to pass a literacy test, and barring virtually all immigration from Asia. The activities of the Ku Klux Klan, founded in 1915, would reach their greatest support by 1920, and their voice echoed that of restrictionists who denounced immigrants as racially inferior, drawing an alarming portrait of an impoverished, criminal, radical, and diseased invading horde. Violent strikes and a rash of bombings followed the outbreak of the war, prompting the Department of Justice to order the arrest of aliens suspected of communist or anarchist sympathies. As immigrants faced hostilities from all sides, Ellis Island's role quickly changed from a depot to that of a detention center. The Red Scare saw hundreds of aliens rounded up and detained at Ellis Island. In addition, over the next year 1,800 German merchant mariners, their ships seized at East Coast ports, were added to the island's population.

"I have become a jailer," Commissioner Frederic C. Howe wrote despondently in 1919 as the wave of anti-immigration hysteria swept the country.

With Atlantic ports and shipping lanes closed to commercial traffic, immigration dropped significantly with the start of World War I. In 1915, 178,000 people were admitted at Ellis Island. By 1919 that number fell to 26,000. With the war's end thousands of refugees from Europe's war damaged areas sailed to the U.S., as did immigrants still holding tickets purchased in 1914. By 1920 immigration had risen again — to a brisk 225,206 arrivals annually. In 1921 the number climbed back to prewar figures of 560,971. For six years the war had delayed the reunion of family and friends, and the postwar immigration crush caught Ellis Island with its resources badly depleted. Experienced staff had been laid off during wartime and the Registry Room, which had been used by the U.S. Army as a ward for wounded servicemen, badly needed repairs and cleaning.

Unfortunately, peace overseas did not bring peace at home. World War I had crystallized anti-immigration sentiment. Nativists continued to criticize the nation's ability to assimilate the flood tide of "human flotsam" and popular tunes such as Neel and Clark's 1923 song *O! Close the Gates* called for a halt to immigration "before this mob from Europe shall drag our Colors down." Restrictionists in Congress remained vigilant in their warnings about the "danger of the melting pot," and on May 19, 1921 succeeded in pressuring President Warren G. Harding into signing the first Quota Act.

The law effectively ended America's open-door policy by setting monthly quotas, limiting admission of each nationality to three percent of its representation in the U.S. Census of 1910. Passengers considered excess quota were automatically excluded. Immigration

Remember Your First Thrill of AMERICAN LIBERTY

YOUR DUTY-*Buy* United States Government *Bonds* 2ⁿᵈ Liberty Loan of 1917

Courtesy Library of Congress

was now more than ever a game of numbers. Steamships jockeyed for position at the mouth of New York Harbor to steam across at the stroke of midnight each month.

The 1924 National Origins Act made further cuts by limiting immigration from any nation to two percent of its representation in the 1890 census. The bill's sponsors made no attempt to conceal its discriminatory intent — directed at restricting "less desirable" immigration from southern and eastern Europe. Very quickly, the gateway to the promised land had all but slammed shut.

The National Origins Act also allowed prospective immigrants to undergo inspection before they left their country of origin, making the trip to Ellis Island unnecessary. Shortly after the Act went into effect, Ellis Island "looked like a deserted village," commented one official. In 1931 Labor Secretary William Doak declared that he would rid the economically depressed nation of "everyone who cannot prove he is a lawful resident here," and in 1932, for the first time ever, more aliens left the country than arrived. By 1937 the island's population had dwindled to about 160 deportees and 30 detained immigrants, mostly Chinese children whose parents, already living in the U.S., had to prove their citizenship.

In the 1940s Ellis Island experienced a renewed flurry of activity. Japanese, German, and Italian citizens were detained on the island during World War II, and later the International Security Act bolstered the detainee population with suspected Communists and Fascists. When Ellis Island's administration moved to an office in Manhattan in 1943, the detained enemy aliens at the station numbered about a thousand. The Coast Guard had also taken up residence on the island, using the main Hospital complex for office and storage space, but by 1949 officials were already discussing closing the immigration depot.

Photo by Joe Luman © Terrell Creative

▲ *The Great Hall*

Ellis Island was becoming too costly to run — in 1953 the island's staff numbered roughly 250, to serve approximately 230 detained immigrants. A 1954 Justice Department ruling, which gave detained aliens parole until their cases could be heard by a ruling board, finally closed Ellis Island's doors on November 19. Its last resident, detainee Arne Peterson, a seaman who overstayed his shore leave, was granted parole and ferried back to the mainland.

Not like the brazen giant of Greek fame,
With conquering limbs astride from land to land;
Here at our sea-washed, sunset gates shall stand
A might woman with a torch whose flame
Is the imprisoned lightning, and her name
Mother of Exiles. From her beacon-hand
Glows world-wide welcome; her mild eyes command
The air-bridged that twin cities frame.
"Keep ancient lands, your storied pomp!" cries she
With silent lips. "Give me your tired, your poor,
Your huddled masses yearning to breathe free,
The wretched refuse of your teeming shore.
Send these, the homeless, temptest-tost to me,
I lift up my lamp beside the golden door!"

— Emma Lazarus, 1883

Photo by Joe Luman © Terrell Creative

▲ Statue of Liberty

▲ *Statue of Liberty with New York Skyline*

Photo by Joe Luman © Terrell Creative

Chapter Three
ELLIS ISLAND RESTORED

Restoration of Ellis Island's Main Building was the most extensive of any single building in the United States. Often compared to the refurbishment of Versailles in France, the project took eight years to complete at a cost of 156 million dollars. Opened September 10, 1990, the Ellis Island Immigration Museum is New York City's fourth largest and receives two million visitors annually — twice as many as entered here in 1907, Ellis Island's peak immigration year. The Immigration Museum's five permanent exhibits contain 5,000 artifacts and hundreds of photographs which trace the history of Ellis Island and the story of American immigration. The museum also incorporates the American Immigrant Wall of Honor, a listing of over 600,000 immigrants' names displayed along Ellis Island's seawall.

From anarchist (Emma Goldman) to pianist (Irving Berlin), from mobster ("Lucky" Luciano) to mayor (New York's Abraham Beame), and from inventor (Igor Sikorsky) to film star (Rudolph Valentino), immigrants added the threads of their lives, whether good or bad, to the nation's fabric. Over 100 million Americans, some forty percent of the country's population, can trace their ancestry in the United States to a man, woman, or child who passed from a steamship to a ferry to the inspection lines in the great Registry Room at Ellis Island.

◄ *Inside Ellis Island's Main Building during restoration*

Photo © Klaus Schnitzer

◄ *Although the Main Building's foundations were in sound condition, its interior walls had sucked up harbor moisture like a sponge. Ceilings had collapsed; walls crumbled at the touch. Some thirty thousand square feet of rotting wooden floors were torn up. To dry the building out, engineers used huge generator-powered furnaces to pump up warm air through thousands of feet of flexible tubing strung throughout the building's rooms — a process which took over two years.*

Photo © Klaus Schnitzer

Not surprisingly, the General Services Administration described Ellis Island as "one of the most famous landmarks in the world" when it tried to sell the island as surplus Federal property in the 1950s. Along with a chunk of history, the buyer would receive thirty-five buildings, two huge water tanks, the ferryboat *Ellis Island*, and thousands of feet of chain link fence left over from the island's days as an enemy and alien detention center.

Advertised in numerous newspapers, the island drew dozens of prospective bids. Suggestions included an atomic research center, a gambling casino, an amusement park, a slaughterhouse, a women's prison, and "the perfect city of tomorrow." No bid was high enough, however, and no sale was made. The doors remained locked, the buildings empty.

Photo © Klaus Schnitzer

▲ *As restoration progressed, workers discovered graffiti left by the immigrants, hidden beneath successive layers of paint on the building's walls. Scratched into the original plaster were names and initials, dating from 1900 to 1954, accompanied by poems, portraits, religious symbols, and cartoons of birds, flowers, and people. Some images were written in pencil, others in the blue chalk the medical inspectors used. Also inscribed were words of heartache. "Damned is the day I left my homeland," wrote one Italian hand, and in Greek, sad and angry fingers scrawled, "Blast you America with your much money who took the Greeks away from their race." To save these telling accounts of the immigrants' frustration, joy, and perseverance, a fine arts conservator used methods developed to preserve the frescoes of Italy.*

Photo © Klaus Schnitzer

▲ *The Registry Room's original plaster ceiling had been severely damaged in 1916 by the explosion of munition barges set afire by German saboteurs on New Jersey's Black Tom Wharf, a mile away. The ceiling was rebuilt in 1917 by Rafael Guastavino, a Spanish immigrant who had arrived with his little boy in the United States in 1881. Guastavino also brought with him ancient Catalonian building techniques, and together he and his son developed a self-supporting system of interlocking terra-cotta tiles that proved light, strong, fireproof, and economical. During the Registry Room's restoration, when the ceiling was inspected and cleaned, only seventeen of the 28,832 tiles originally set by the Guastavinos had to be replaced.*

◄ *During this time, restoration crews took inventory of everything in the Main Building — from radiators and toilets to sinks and electric fans — in an attempt to use as many original fixtures as possible. The Main Building's Registry Room, which had been the principal waystation for most immigrants processed at Ellis Island, provided a benchmark for restoration. The time period from 1918-1924 was selected as it coincided with the construction date of the Hall's 56-foot high barrel-vaulted ceilings and peak immigration years.*

▼ *Various techniques were used to bring back the Main Building's original appearance. One such technique was sand painting the walls of the Registry Room so that they would give an impression of stone. The work was done by hand and, pictured here is some of the scaffolding that enabled craftsmen to reach areas of the wall without having to use ladders.*

Photo © Klaus Schnitzer

For ten years Ellis Island stood vacant, subject to vandals and looters who made off with anything they could carry, from doorknobs to filing cabinets. The building's Beaux-Arts copper ornamentation deteriorated. Snow swirled through broken windows, roofs leaked, and weeds sprang up in corridors, growing in the footprints of anxious immigrants long gone. Ellis Island was forgotten, swallowed by the fierce weather of New York Harbor.

In October of 1964 Stewart Udall, Secretary of the Interior for President Lyndon Johnson, visited Ellis Island and recognized it as a vital part of America's heritage. Udall urged President Johnson to rescue the island and preserve a piece of America's past by placing the island in the permanent care of the National Park Service. Ellis Island became part of Statue of Liberty National Monument in 1965.

Photo © Klaus Schnitzer

➤ *Originally Ellis Island had little vegetation but over the years various plants were introduced. As a result, the island now has a fairly rich variety of plantings, including the lawn, flowers and London plane trees. The trees, some of which appear in this picture, were added to the landscape in the 1930s.*

Rebuilding the seawall — to keep the island's landfill from slipping into the harbor — became the first preservation task. Congress appropriated one million dollars for its upkeep. Yet Ellis Island remained a magnificent wreck. In 1976 the dilapidated Main Building opened to the public, and more than fifty thousand visitors a year toured the historic site until the island again closed in 1984. Public awareness and concern over Ellis Island's disrepair had inspired private citizens to mount a campaign to save what was left of its buildings. The Statue of Liberty/Ellis Island Foundation was created in 1982 in an effort to restore both monuments, and in the early 1980s, funded by private donations, work began on Ellis Island.

Workers also focused on restoring the Main Building's exterior. Years of exposure had painted it black with soot and the dirt of pollution. The building's granite foundation was washed clean with a solution of chemicals and water, and high-pressure steam jets polished its delicate limestone trim.

Photo by Joe Luman © Terrell Creative

◄ *Seen here is the steel and glass canopy that covers the walkway and entrance of the Main Building. The original canopy stood in the same place from 1903 to 1931.*

▼ *The ferry house was constructed in the 1930s to replace the previous one that had been badly damaged in a windstorm. The building, which is currently being restored, was divided into various rooms. The largest room was a large passenger waiting hall. The Customs Service inspectors occupied an area of the building, while other rooms were allotted to the captain, engineers and crew of the ferryboat.*

The National Park Service's 1978 study of the Main Building revealed that only fifty percent of the original copper ornamentation remained in place. Using surviving pieces as models, workers replaced the cornices and cupolas that had disappeared or deteriorated. New copper domes, installed piece by piece, were crowned with spires placed by helicopter.

The tiled turreted Main Building once again welcomes with a grand gesture. The Immigration Museum's exhibits educate rather than intimidate — and open the eyes of visitors to the complex and often contradictory emotions immigrants felt when they arrived on America's shores. Ellis Island symbolized America's majesty, but also its willingness to reject the unwanted. As immigrants continue to flow into the United States, Ellis Island speaks not only of past promises, but also of the future.

Photo by Joe Luman © Terrell Creative

Photo by Joe Luman © Terrell Creative

▲ This exhibit shows the ferryboat Ellis Island in the days when it actively served immigrants released from Ellis Island and the station's employees, missionaries and immigrant aid workers.

◄ Called "Millions on the Move: Worldwide Migration," this exhibit shows the main streams of migration from the countries of origin to various destinations over the last few centuries. The destinations include the United States, Canada, Brazil, Spanish America, the West Indies, Australia, New Zealand and South Africa, while the regions sending emigrants include Europe, Africa, Asia and the Middle East.

➤ "The American Flag" exhibit is located in the Peopling of America Gallery. The flag is a mosaic of more than 750 Americans from all of the country's ethnic groups. Seen from the opposite side, the American Flag's ethnic faces change to the dazzling red, white and blue of Old Glory.

▲ *Another aspect of immigration treated in the exhibit, "Where We Came From: Sources of Immigration." The exhibit shows the statistical figures for immigration from the different quarters of the world at intervals of twenty years.*

➤ *"A Two Way Street: Immigration versus Emigration" reveals that America has not only been a recipient of migrants but that it has also seen people leave its own shores for other countries. Many emigrants leaving the United States had previously immigrated here. Approximately one third of America's foreign migrants eventually returned to their homelands or emigrated to another country entirely.*

Photo by Joe Luman © Terrell Creative

The First Americans: Indian Groups

Photo by Joe Luman © Terrell Creative

◄ *"The First Americans: Indian Groups" exhibit shows the distribution of the American Indian nations and tribes throughout the continent at the beginning of European colonization in the New World. Many of North America's native peoples later migrated to other sections of the continent, often in reaction to the new arrivals from Europe and Africa.*

Photo by Joe Luman © Terrell Creative

➤ Called "A Changing Pattern: Male and Female Immigration Trends" focuses on the differences of the sexes as foreign migrants to the United States. Before 1914, males dominated the statistics of most nationalities entering the country. They often came to earn enough money to return home or to bring over other family members. Although most women immigrants came to join the men, some, such as the Irish, Swedes, Germans, and Polish Catholics often came to seek work on their own account.

➤ Highlighting the westward expansion of the United States from its east coast base, this exhibit depicts the stages of that expansion which advanced sometimes through military conflict and sometimes through diplomacy.

Photo by Joe Luman © Terrell Creative

Photo by Joe Luman © Terrell Creative

➤ *Perhaps one quarter of Americans today can trace their family history to at least one person who entered Ellis Island Immigration Station and rode a ferry.*

▼ *Sculptor Philip Ratner exemplified the difficulties of immigrants through his many statuettes which are on permanent exhibit at Ellis Island.*

Courtesy Library of Congress

Photo by Joe Luman © Terrell Creative

Photo by Joe Luman © Terrell Creative

Photo by Joe Luman © Terrell Creative

▲ *The museum incorporates the American Immigrant Wall of Honor®, a listing of more than 600,000 immigrants' names.*

Photo by Joe Luman © Terrell Creative

For today's visitor, the journey to Ellis Island begins as it did for twelve million immigrants who entered here in the early twentieth century. The ferry swings away from the dock, leaving behind New York's distinctive skyline as the Statue of Liberty raises her gleaming torch across the busy harbor. Arriving ferry passengers file out toward Ellis Island's impressive brick and limestone Main Building. Inside, the Baggage Room houses a collection of baskets, trunks, and suitcases brought by immigrants. Upstairs, visitors guide themselves through the massive Registry Room, meticulously restored to its appearance in 1918-1924. Exhibits on three floors trace Ellis Island's history and the complex story of American immigration. A documentary film and optional audio tours are available.

Ellis Island is administered by Statue of Liberty National Monument, National Park Service. Ferries servicing Ellis and Liberty Islands leave at regular intervals from Battery Park in Manhattan, and from Liberty State Park in New Jersey. A gift shop and food service are located on the first floor.

▲ *Part of the legacy of Ellis Island is not only the millions of Americans who trace a relative that passed through it as an immigrant, but also the many successful immigrants whom it's spawned. Among these are cosmetologist Max Factor from Russia, actress Claudette Colbert from France, chef Ettore Boiardi (Chef Boyardee) from Italy, dancer Pearl Primus from Trinidad, bandleader Xavier Cugat from Cuba, singer Alfred Piccaver from England, and author H.T. Tsiang from China.*